THE CARDLESS

TAROT

Dedicated to
everyone who
wants to write
their own destiny.

ILLUSTRATED BY
MAGDALENA KACZAN

THE CARDLESS

TAROT

CHOOSE YOUR OWN DESTINY TAROT READINGS

KERRY WARD

Hardie Grant

BOOKS

A unique *cardless* tarot experience.

Readings for people who don't have cards or are on-the-go.

Contents

Introduction

I have been reading, teaching and creating tarot for over 25 years and my mission is to make it as easy, accessible and fun as possible. I want everybody to own a deck and read their own cards and enjoy the tarot's amazing repository of human knowledge, wisdom and life experience. But that depth of knowledge may not be for everyone and I am constantly on the lookout for ways to bring tarot to a wider audience.

Just to briefly give some context for beginners, the tarot – just like an ordinary deck of cards – is divided into four suits; in the case of tarot, these are Cups, Wands, Swords and Pentacles. Each suit contains cards One to Ten, plus a Page, Knight, Queen and King. These are called the minor arcana. In addition, there are 22 major arcana, called the power cards, which all have specific names.

The inspiration for this book came to me when I dug out my old 'Fighting Fantasy' (choose your own adventure) books to share with my niece, Billie. I started to re-read them and I remembered how much I loved that format of storytelling. I thought that this could be applied to tarot readings, allowing access to people who don't have cards or who want something on-the-go, something immediate and quick, or who are perhaps just dipping their toe into the realm of tarot reading and divination.

That evolved into this entirely new proposition in understanding tarot and I hope that it will enable many more people to experience the tarot and see if they like it – without even having to buy cards or learn the system – because this is a unique, cardless tarot.

How to use this book

Step 1:
You pick a question or theme that is pertinent to your life at that moment. The question you ask determines who will guide you on the next step.

Step 2:
You will be introduced to your guide and the symbolism of their realm through the medium of storytelling. You will share the story of your life and make an instinctive selection of a symbolic object from within their realm.

    The symbolic object you select will lead you to your specific reading.

Step 3:
Consider carefully the reading meant for you in that moment and determine how to put the advice into practice.

    You don't have to learn all the interpretations of the cards because you'll find all the readings waiting for you in this book; all you need to do is turn to the designated page.

The guides in this book, who talk to you about the questions or theme you've chosen, are all characters from the major arcana of the tarot. These are the power icons, the unseen forces, and they are here to help you find your answers. You can revisit them as often as you wish, there are many different readings to choose from, and they should each help you form a new plan of action that will guide you towards your destiny.

This book is perfect for anyone who is completely new to tarot, those who are just curious, someone looking for an on-the-spot, pick-me-up answer or reading, those hoping to use tarot as a meditation aid, and those testing the waters of this vast esoteric playground.

I truly hope that you enjoy the book, the experience and the answers you receive. They come from my heart with my best wishes for your future endeavours and efforts.

Kerry

**This book is perfect
for anyone who is
completely new to tarot.**

Step 1:

Your Question

If you know anything about tarot, it is probably the fact that each reading begins with a question – and that is fundamental to how it works.

arot does not give you prescriptive 'do this, do that' instructions. It is designed to open doors, to lead you down pathways, perhaps ones you have not walked before. So the first step is to approach the tarot with a singular, meaningful question. The more precise your question, the more targeted your answer is likely to be.

In this book, I have created the questions for you, so you simply pick the one that resonates with you right now. Maybe even just the one your eye is drawn to because that might mean the Universe is nudging you in that direction and this is what you need to explore on that particular day. Each question is presented to you by a guide from the major arcana of the tarot (the power cards). Meet the guide associated with your question, then choose one of five symbols that you will discover in their domain to lead you to the answer to your question. Turn to the designated page for your reading. The readings have been created specifically for this book, using a 78-card tarot deck so you experience a true, full reading.

Timing and Interpretation

There are no rules as to how often you can do your tarot readings – you can establish your own time-frame – but do keep that in your mind in relation to your interpretation. These readings are designed primarily to give you an overview of the coming months of your life and to help you to make significant decisions, so you might allocate time once a month. When reading for clients, I wouldn't recommend they visit more than once a month unless they were addressing totally separate, and unrelated, life areas.

If you find them helpful and want to do readings more frequently, you can tighten your expectations. For example, if you are thinking of moving home in the next months, the advice that 'sometimes a different environment completely refreshes our own personality and outlook' might inspire you to take the plunge and look at homes some distance away. If this is a daily reading, it might be all you

Choose a Question to Ask the Tarot

We have used the wisdom of the tarot deck to frame questions relating to nine of the power cards. There is enough scope and variety in the questions to give you insight into all areas of your life using just these nine questions. Ask one question at a time and focus on that question.

You can return to the questions as often as you like, and you'll find yourself making different choices for your guide, even when the topic is similar, as your circumstances shift. The questions are designed in such a way that they will mould to your individual requirements so they are uniquely suited to you. Choose the one you are most drawn to.

Which question would you like to ask?

Turn to the relevant page to be introduced to the most appropriate guide for your journey.

Step 2

Your Guides and Their Domains

Each of the questions in the previous section will lead you to one of our nine tarot guides who will accompany you on your journey.

Follow your question to its guide in this section, experience where they live and share your life story with them. Then choose a symbolic item from their realm to take you to the tarot reading for your question.

As you read about your guide and their realm, bring your own story to the foreground in relation to your question. Think about key relevant points in your childhood or your life so far that influenced you greatly; about the challenges you have faced and obstacles you have overcome. Tell the story of your achievements and successes, the strengths you possess and the qualities you lack. Weave it into a narrative that becomes an honest and thoughtful story of your life, such as you'd share with this guide, such as you'd think was pertinent to the question they are helping you with.

As you talk to your guide, immerse yourself completely so you almost feel as though you were watching yourself in a movie. Become part of your own story and, at the same time, be in the moment as you tell your story to your guide.

Meditation

If you have experience of meditation, you will be familiar with the feeling of immersing yourself in another realm. If that is unfamiliar to you, you may want to try some simple relaxation exercises before you do your first reading.

- Sit or lie comfortably in a quiet place and breathe deeply, making sure you exhale fully. Continue with a deep and relaxed, natural breathing pattern.
- Gradually work through your body, tensing and then releasing groups of muscles in turn: your face, neck, arms and hands, core, legs and feet. Concentrate on your body and leave everything else behind.
- Feel completely relaxed for however long you feel comfortable, then bring yourself back to reality. You should feel calm but energized.

The idea is to allow yourself to be completely relaxed and let your intuition take over.

Visualization

With practice, you can learn to take your meditation a step further and really visualize a scene in your mind's eye and bring it to life in your imagination to experience almost as if you were there. There is plenty of information out there to explain how it works. If you practise, you will find it progressively easier to visualize your story or your journey as you experience it.

The Questions and the Guides

Turn to the relevant page to be introduced to the most appropriate guide for your journey.

What new beginning am I destined to initiate now?

The Fool
(page 27)

What is my unique talent or power that I can unleash now?

The Magician
(page 29)

What do I *need* to know about my life right now?

The High Priestess
(page 31)

The Fool's Threshold
Unlock a fresh start

The question that brought you here:
What new beginning am I destined to initiate now?

You find yourself yearning for a fresh start, a clean slate, a new chapter, so you have come to see the Fool, the tarot's patron saint of new beginnings. The Fool's realm is a stark, windswept clifftop overlooking a dark, churning ocean below. The air is bracing and sharp.

Suddenly, from above in the sky, you hear a voice calling your name. You look up to see the silhouette of the Fool shifting and moving in the clouds above. He tells you that to reveal the nature and first step of your fresh start, you need to prove your commitment to it by leaping from the cliff! He reassures you that your physical body will remain in repose, protected and safe, on the clifftop; it is your mental and emotional self that leave your body and take this leap. And he tells you that, as you fall, the clouds will reveal a symbol meant only for you. It is this symbol that will unlock your new chapter.

With a deep breath and a shake of your limbs, you run towards the cliff edge and fling yourself over. The wind lifts you and, momentarily, you are weightless, flying, in sync with the airy elements supporting you. It feels amazing.

As you feel your weight begin to pull you down, you flip and face the clouds. They swirl and shift to reform into a symbol. It imprints on your mind. You close your eyes as your descent speeds up and, with a final thud, you feel yourself reconnect with your physical body. You open your eyes and find yourself still standing back on the clifftop, next to the Fool, who is smiling encouragingly at you.

'Tell me what the clouds showed you,' he says. And you do.

Which cloud symbol did you see?
The boat (page 50)
The compass (page 58)
The daisy (page 68)
The dog (page 70)
The feather (page 76)
Turn to the relevant page to find your reading.

The Magician's Chamber

Unleash your talent and power

The question that brought you here:
What is my unique talent or power that I can unleash now?

You have decided that you are ready to acknowledge, appreciate and unleash your personal talent or power. You are at a point in your life when you wish to align with your authentic and unique skills and experience. You wish to create, establish and build something new. And it all starts within. It all starts with recognizing the magic that already lives inside you, which just needs time and focus to activate and bring it to its full potential.

And so you find yourself seeking an audience with the Magician. She is a trickster, a sage, a wise fool, an inventor and a sorcerer of transformative magic. You have travelled a long way to see her, through a dark, enchanted forest, and the journey gave you time to think about where your inner magic may reside.

The Magician bids you to take a seat in her fascinating, star-lit spell chamber, which perches at the top of an ivy-covered turret. A merry fire crackles in the hearth casting leaping shadows up the walls and over the Magician's earnest face. She asks you to tell her of your ruminations about the source and nature of your power and talent. You recall what you were good at when you were in school, what hobbies you enjoyed, how you entertained yourself in play, what you wished to become when you grew up.

She nods encouragingly and responds that our personal power is implanted within us from birth but can take a lifetime to fathom out, believe in, and learn to use in everyday life – especially in making a good living.

She bids you to look over her shelves and choose a magic object from amongst the books, that chimes with you. When you pick up this object it will resonate to the hidden talent or power within you and reveal this to you.

Examine the shelves and choose your object. Is it?
The flowers (page 78)
The infinity symbol (page 86)
The serpent statue (page 110)
The wand (page 128)
The robe (page 130)
Turn to the relevant page to find your reading.

29

The High Priestess' Temple

Discover what you need to know

The question that brought you here:
What do I need to know about my life right now?

You are aware of unseen forces at work in your life and you feel the Universe has knowledge or instruction for you that will make a big difference to your future pathway. You want to tap into the unseen, the unknown, the hidden, and therefore you are seeking an audience with the High Priestess. She is the keeper of secret knowledge, the guardian of the window into the worlds beyond our own, the bridge between the seen and the unseen.

She resides in her temple which is nestled in a cavern hollowed down in the depths of a lush, sun-baked hillside. As you step from the heat of the day into the temple you are struck by the cool air and quiet atmosphere. A swirling, scented vapour hangs in the air. You walk through the vapour towards a throne set up high where the High Priestess is seated.

She sits between white and black pillars with the veil of the temple flowing behind her; it is embroidered with palms and pomegranates. The vestments are gauzy, casting a shimmering radiance. She has a lunar crescent lying at her feet, a horned moon diadem crown on her head, and a large solar cross on the breast of her gown. She is toying with an old scroll in her hands.

She smiles at you. In that moment, the swirling vapour starkly intensifies, and she disappears into the mist, hidden now from view. The scent of smoke tinged with bright pomegranate is making you drowsy. A voice in your mind (her voice), calmly asks you to visualize what you remember of her and her temple. When you fix that object in your mind's eye, the knowledge that is meant for you, and you alone, will be revealed to you.

What part of the High Priestess' appearance resonated most with you?
The cross on her gown (page 60)
Her horned moon diadem crown (page 84)
Her lunar crescent (page 94)
The scroll (page 108)
The veil of the temple (page 126)
Turn to the relevant page to find your reading.

The Empress' Paradise

Meet your next lover

The question that brought you here:
How will I meet my next love?

Your love life is playing on your mind and you feel you are ready to meet someone new. A trip to the paradise realm of the Empress will help you to understand who your next great love is and how to find them.

The Empress lives beside a tropical lagoon beneath a tall, rippling waterfall which spills down into a lush paradise of orchids, roses, vines and palm trees. The Empress likes to sit on a rock and feel the spray of water cool her body. It is here that you meet her and tell her your questions.

She listens carefully and smiles. She tells you that love is the greatest gift we can give and receive in this life, although it also has a double edge and can wound deeply when it fades or is misplaced. She tells you that you can manifest a true love by creating a vision of it, asking the Universe to bring it to you, and then believing in this vision and acting as though it were in your life already. How you treat yourself teaches others how to treat you and will attract complementary energies. Take good care of your health, wealth and wellbeing. Prioritize your needs. Improve, grow, develop, take on challenges. This is the best preparation for a dream lover.

She lays out five objects before you. Each one represents a potential future lover for you, and all are in play because there is no such thing as one soul mate or love. You have many options and, should one run its course, then you are welcome to return and choose again. She asks you to select an object to take back and place in your window as a beacon for this next partner to be drawn towards.

You gaze at the objects. Now you must decide which one you will take home as your love beacon.
The heart brooch (page 82)
The pearl necklace (page 98)
The sheaf of wheat (page 112)
The wreath (page 132)
The zodiac crown (page 134)
Turn to the relevant page to find your reading.

The Emperor's Spire
Create your next major goal

The question that brought you here:
What is my next game-changing priority, ambition or goal?

You are ready to set yourself an inspiring fresh challenge. You are seeking a new goal or ambition to aim for, work on, and invest energy into. You need to clarify it, plan it, schedule its achievement and understand the rewards or results you expect to reap. To focus and refine it, you have decided to visit the most powerful person in the major arcana kingdom: the Emperor.

You have trekked through a perilous mountain range to his fortress high up in the peaks, its spires surrounded by drifting clouds. In the tallest spire lies the Emperor's throne room and this is where you now sit, facing your ally and adviser.

All around him are trophies, tokens and symbols of his success, conquests, victories and adventures. A beautiful globe hangs from the ceiling, lit within by an orange glow which warms the room. His golden throne is decorated with rams' heads. Bright, polished armour, inscribed with many sigils of luck, wisdom and divinity hang from the walls. Swords encrusted with precious gems are lined up beneath the arched window, where on the sill sits his crown, its jewels casting multi-coloured lights all around the walls. The Emperor uses every asset, every advantage, every strength and tool, to his advantage. He knows how to win. But he knows you need to know what you're fighting for, and why.

After telling him of your journey and quests so far in life, he sits back, steeples his fingers and looks at you over the top of his hands. He says that your next ambition or goal will be the one revealed by the answer to one simple question. You eagerly enquire what the question is, and he smiles.

'That, in part, is the real trick here. I will leave you in my throne room, my seat of success and victory. Wander, ponder and imagine. Dare to dream. Let your ideas solidify around an object in this room and, when you're ready, reach out and touch it. When you do, the question you need to answer to clarify your next goal will be revealed.' The Emperor shakes your hand and leaves you in his throne room.

You look around and decide which object you are going to touch.
The armour (page 46)
The crown (page 64)
The hanging globe (page 80)
The ram-adorned throne (page 102)
The swords (page 120)
Turn to the relevant page to find your reading.

35

The Hierophant's Sanctum

Understand your most pressing life lesson

The question that brought you here:
What life lesson can I build on right now?

Life has been challenging but you have faced and tackled what needed to be done, and feel like the darkness is yielding to a new dawn. Before you begin afresh, you wish to process, understand and extract wisdom from what has passed.

You have come to see the Hierophant, the tarot's authority in wisdom and knowledge. What he doesn't know, he knows how to find out. You have come to ask for his guidance in unveiling your key life lesson at this moment.

You have been sitting in his richly decorated study for some time, discussing the situation and assessing what you've learnt, regretted, felt pride in achieving, and wished were different. The Hierophant has listened carefully, often closing his eyes to absorb your narrative into his own inner world and turn it over in his mind's eye.

He tells you to turn and face the beautiful, handmade stained glass window casting wonderful shapes and colourful shadows all around the room. There are five panels in the window, each depicting a particular symbol.

He asks you to close your eyes and ask for the life lesson of the hardships or tests you have endured.

He starts to chant at a frequency that relaxes you, and your mind turns inwards. You replay the events and examine them from other angles, you notice your feelings and you release them.

Suddenly the Hierophant claps his hands, demands that you open your eyes and gaze at the window. The panel's symbol that your eye first notices is the key to your lesson. Tell him what it is, and he will reveal what you need to know now.

You open your eyes and look at the window. Which symbol do you tell him you see first?

The crossed keys (page 62)
The entwined rose and lily (page 74)
The kneeling monks (page 88)
The sceptre (page 106)
The three-tiered crown (page 122)
Turn to the relevant page to find your reading.

The Hermit's Cave
Seek enlightenment

The question that brought you here:
What do I need to understand about myself?

You are seeking enlightenment, knowledge, truth and education. You are looking to illuminate corners of your mind with fresh information, stimulus or altered angles of perception, and enter a different chapter marked by what you now know or have come to understand. Wisdom is gained by enduring and processing experiences, but knowledge is gained by active pursuit.

And so you find yourself seeking an audience with the Hermit. He is a philosopher, a deep thinker, a master of many skills and disciplines. There is little under the stars that he doesn't understand or know how to access. You have scaled the heights of a tall and imposing mountain range to reach the Hermit's cave, which nestles into a ledge on the highest peak, far from the world. The climb has given you time to ponder what it is you wish to ask and where you seek enlightenment.

The Hermit greets you as if he knew you were coming and bids you to sit on the floor of his cave, which is illuminated by a glowing lantern, revealing glittering obsidian, crystal-hewed walls, a dark, deep pool at the back of the cave which echoes with running water trickling down somewhere deeper into the mountain. The Hermit's cloak and staff lie at his feet.

He looks deep into your eyes and says in a low voice.

'I know the nature of the knowledge you seek, and I can give you the tools you need to dig for and carve it out from yourself, so that you and you alone can understand its message.'

He stands and casts his arm out around the glittering cave.

'Choose the thing that first caught, and then held, your attention when you entered my cave. This object possesses the key to the knowledge you seek.'

Examine the cave and choose your object. Is it?
The cloak (page 56)
The crystal walls (page 66)
The lantern (page 90)
The mountain pool (page 96)
The staff (page 118)
Turn to the relevant page to find your reading.

39

The Wheel of Fortune
Reveal an unexpected event on the horizon

The question that brought you here:
What changes lie ahead for me?

The only constant in life is change. Sometimes we dread it, sometimes we endure it, sometimes we seek it out. Today is a day for the latter. You are hoping for change, transformation, renewal, different energy and opportunity ... and so you stand before the Wheel of Fortune. This is where destinies are made.

This wheel represents unexpected changes. Once spun, you put in motion a chain of events that you can't see the full extent of. You are placing your future in the hands of fate and, although there may be ups and downs, the general outcome will always be a positive one.

The wheel is vast and colourful, intricately designed, with beautiful carvings and symbols from many different cultures and continents. We are universally linked in our relationship with change, ageing, growth, maturity and, ultimately, death. We all live in shared life cycles. We all follow a similar path.

You step forward, closer to the wheel, thinking about your life as it is right now and what you wish was different. You imagine a future where this area of your world has transformed. And you make a wish.

Holding that desire in mind, you push the wheel. It creaks and slowly starts to shift. You lean in and push even harder, feeling its enormous weight starting to drop and the clockwork machinations within it starting to whirl and click into action. The wheel picks up pace and you step back as it suddenly twirls into a fast and whirring spin.

The wheel turns. The colours merge. The shapes and symbols blur.

And then it slows, grinding to a creaking halt. Whatever magic it has generated and exuded has now been passed onto you and entered your life's landscape. The spell is cast.

When the wheel stops, notice which symbol its hand is pointing to because this reveals the fate now awaiting you. Is it?
The bull (page 52)
The eagle (page 72)
The lion (page 92)
The snake (page 114)
The sphinx (page 116)
Turn to the relevant page to find your reading.

The Devil's Underworld
Meet your shadow self

The question that brought you here:
What message does my shadow self yearn to reveal to me?

You know you have demons, the presence of a shadow self, a side of your character that you shun. And you feel it's time, at last, to face it and resolve the divide between you. To do this, you have entered the Devil's Underworld, a liminal space where you can meet your shadow self safely and on equal terms.

You have descended into the Earth's core beneath a smouldering volcano, and find yourself in a dark cavern facing a mottled and blackened mirror which is hewn into the cave wall. You step towards the mirror and gaze into it. Your reflection shows that, behind you, swirls a purple, misty void. You hear, coming from deep within it, the sound of footsteps approaching, and you recognize them as your shadow self's gait. You know it well because it has walked beside you many times.

The footsteps get louder and nearer and the purple mist in the mirror clears to reveal your shadow self, standing just behind your left shoulder.

Turning to face it, you feel no fear, only curiosity and sympathy. It wants to talk. It wants to tell you its story, where it came from, what awakens it, and what it is sorry for doing to you. It wants you to help it find peace. Show your shadow self your authentic understanding and compassion. Shame cannot survive in the face of true empathy.

What does your shadow self say? Listen carefully.

When you've finished, thank it for the visit, and let it retreat. Take a deep breath and turn from the mirror. You notice, on the ground, it has left you a token.

Which token did your shadow self leave you?
The bat wing (page 48)
The chain (page 54)
The pentacle (page 100)
The ring (page 104)
The torch (page 124)
Turn to the relevant page to find your reading.

Step 3: Your Readings

The following readings are organized alphabetically by the name of the object you chose in your guide's realm. That object represents the essence of the reading you needed to receive at that time. Flick through the following pages to find the object and consider your reading.

    Don't be surprised if you ask the same question more than once and reach a different reading. Life is in constant flux and you will find that viewing the same issue from different standpoints is immensely valuable.

    Opposite the heading you will find the three tarot cards most associated with the symbol and which form the basis of the reading.

You Chose the Armour in the Emperor's Spire

KNIGHT OF COINS

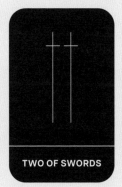

TWO OF SWORDS

KING OF SWORDS

The question that brought you here: What is my next game-changing priority, ambition or goal?

The question that you need to answer to realize your next goal is 'what is the most powerful, life-changing decision that is in my hands to make at the present moment?'.

The Knight of Coins shows that the objective here is to bring certainty and surety to your world by making the biggest decision on your plate right now, even if it's a 'no' or a 'no action required' decision. Make it conscious and then pour all your reserves of power into what you've consciously decided to do or to prioritize. This is about protecting what you love, building what you have, creating stability.

The Two of Swords reveals that your guiding light or principle is to be decisive, direct, clear and confident. Make decision-making an art form, a game, a super-power. Research the risks, mitigate them. Debate the pros and cons. Project ahead into possible scenarios. Answer unanswered questions. And, ultimately, sleep on your decision before making it. Any unresolved emotions will emerge at that point. Address them.

The King of Swords confirms that your reward is the ability to redesign your life, create a new future, craft a pathway that leads to the life you dream of living. Everything starts somewhere – usually in our imagination, activated by a bold choice. This is that time; this is the embryo of that next major life chapter and pathway.

47

You Chose the Bat Wing in the Devil's Underworld

STRENGTH

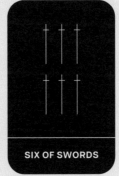
SIX OF SWORDS

QUEEN OF COINS

The question that brought you here: What message does my shadow self yearn to reveal to me?

Your shadow self's origin is Strength. There was a time you were tested or challenged and felt that you fell short, and that ignited the emergence of this shadow side to protect you from ever failing or falling short again. This self can talk you out of leaving comfort zones, project doubt and uncertainty, and undermine your confidence. This shadow self is motivated by safety and surety, but it restricts your ability to grow and develop to your full potential.

It is triggered by the Six of Swords. When it feels you are moving beyond the realms of what it feels is 'safety', it awakens and creates fear or projected obstacles to try to bring you back into the fold. You must override these interferences. The Six of Swords shows you *are* ready to move into fresh landscapes and take on new challenges – this shadow self's fears are groundless.

You can bring peace and healing to your shadow self with the Queen of Coins. Be maternal and motherly towards your inner fearful side. Reassure it that all will be well and you can handle whatever comes. Distract it with a treat, with praise and entertainment. Quell its fears. Show the practical, tangible steps you have taken towards mitigating risks or problems. Be practical, take action.

You Chose the Boat in the Fool's Threshold

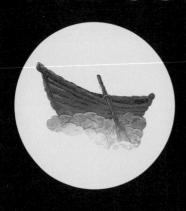

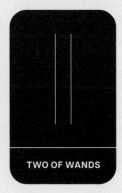

SEVEN OF CUPS **THE EMPRESS** **TWO OF WANDS**

The question that brought you here: What new beginning am I destined to initiate now?

The nature of your fresh start is revealed by the Seven of Cups. You are being given access to your wildest, most heartfelt daydreams and the chance to draw one of them into your real life. This new beginning comes entirely from your imagination, your fantasy life. It's time to manifest what you dream about, this is it!

The outcome or goal of this journey is shared by The Empress. This journey is one towards your dream home, your ideal relationship, your perfect family structure, your beautiful lifestyle. Love rules over everything in this world and you are adored, appreciated, needed and valued here. Whatever your vision of a happy home is, it's time to make it a reality.

Your first step is introduced by the Two of Wands: focus and prioritization. You can't magic a whole world out of nothing overnight, but you can start to lay the foundations. Once they're strong and secure, you can build faster and easier, so begin by clearing away the dead wood, rubble and false roots. Get rid of everything that doesn't serve this vision. Then focus on the one or two things that need to be activated to begin to make it real. Once the momentum builds, things will happen faster than you can imagine. This process can be under way in less than a month!

You Chose the Bull on the Wheel of Fortune

THE DEVIL **WHEEL OF FORTUNE** **ACE OF COINS**

The question that brought you here: What changes lie ahead for me?

The first thing that will change is The Devil. You have the necessary insight, self-awareness, willpower and determination to totally break, dismantle and replace a bad habit, pattern or limiting self-belief. You are escaping a torment, putting away an old demon, leaving behind a cloying behaviour that serves you no good (but you've been powerless to resist until now). This is a positive leap forwards and it comes from changing a long-standing negative habit or belief.

The purpose of this transformation is the Wheel of Fortune. You recognize this habit or pattern is dictating the shape and trajectory of your life and you're tired of being victim and prey to it. Enough! The Wheel of Fortune is your purpose – total transformation, new landscape and scenery, fresh outlook, different energy and mentality. You are ready for a total clean slate.

The outcome of this process of change is the Ace of Coins. You are facing a year-long (maximum) process of transformation, where each day brings out a positive step forward and a better mood. Your health, wealth, work and home will all be positively impacted. You are laying down new, better, stronger foundations for your life and future. You are creating stability and security. You are taking better care of yourself.

53

You Chose the Chain in the Devil's Underworld

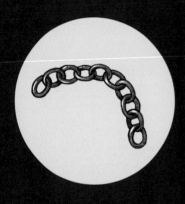

KING OF COINS

FIVE OF CUPS

SEVEN OF CUPS

The question that brought you here: What message does my shadow self yearn to reveal to me?

Your shadow self's origin is the King of Coins. This could be a father figure or totem of authority in your early life, perhaps someone who held the line, was strict, set tough goals or high expectations. Their voice (or even demands) is never that far from you and has morphed into a shadow self that often pushes you to perfection, is never satisfied, and can undermine your confidence or sense of success.

It is triggered by the Five of Cups. When you feel any kind of regret or sadness about something not working out as you originally hoped, you can spiral into a destructive and critical onslaught which focuses on your own failings. It can be brief but intense and it can leave you feeling bad about yourself. We all have regrets at times, but we need to turn them away from the negative to eventually make them positive and healthy when positioned as practical 'lessons' to apply next time around (rather than recriminations we have to absorb).

You can bring peace and healing to your shadow self with the Seven of Cups. This is a mental and imagination game. Your shadow self has to reframe their attitude to regret (whether it be from mistakes, outside events or missed opportunities). Tell your shadow self to dream up the lesson from each tinge of regret, to create a practical plan to stop it happening again or overcome the issue. Be creative. Be visionary. Turn setbacks into opportunities to learn.

55

You Chose the Cloak in the Hermit's Cave

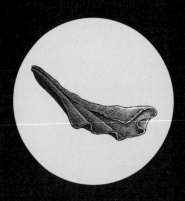

NINE OF CUPS

STRENGTH

EIGHT OF CUPS

The question that brought you here: What do I need to understand about myself?

The nature of the knowledge or enlightenment you seek is the Nine of Cups. You want to know your true heart's desire and unfulfilled promise (that is still within reach). You want a new goal, a motivating ambition, a fresh daydream, a different future. It is comforting to know what we really want. It can intuitively shape our decisions and actions. You have been feeling a little lost without that guiding light. It's time to ignite it.

The pathway to finding this knowledge is Strength. Revisit your story so far, focusing, in particular, on the obstacles, challenges and setbacks you have handled, overcome and learnt from. When you look at the path already navigated, you will have more hope and belief in what you can do in the future. You can reap the rewards of this knowledge. It's likely your dream will be linked to a new trial, challenge, competition or challenging goal. Accept that everything has a price. Set yourself a goal.

The outcome of pursuing, clarifying and understanding this knowledge is the Eight of Cups. You might feel a little disappointed in the things you have on the go at present – as though they are not 'it'. That's okay. They have served a purpose, but if you're to move on and approach your heart's desire, you may need to refocus and release them. Maybe that is the price to pay. Don't fear failure, don't settle for where you're at. You now have a new horizon to aim for.

You Chose the Compass in the Fool's Threshold

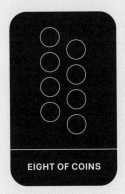

EIGHT OF COINS

QUEEN OF COINS

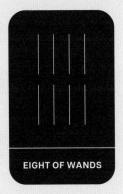

EIGHT OF WANDS

The question that brought you here: What new beginning am I destined to initiate now?

The nature of your fresh start is revealed by the Eight of Coins. This is a long-term pathway which relates to your health, wealth, work or home. You will need to work very hard to make this project a success but every scrap of effort will yield equal rewards. You will extract what you invest, and then some. This is a worthwhile endeavour. This marks a new seven-year chapter.

The outcome or goal of this journey is shared by the Queen of Coins. Riches, prosperity, security, luxury, good health and vitality, recognition and reward. This is the pathway to lasting, sustained success and wellbeing, to your legacy in life. You are ready to become what you were meant to be.

Your first step is introduced by the Eight of Wands. You need to reach out and network. It's who versus what you know in this life that gets you the opportunities and opens the doors. Share your ambitions with everyone – reach out and reconnect. Focus on people who can help or advise, seek guidance. Someone will give you access to the first step, and it will all unfold from there. This will start and take on momentum in the next two months. That period is so important; make sure you have set off on this journey before that time has passed – the window of opportunity is here now.

You Chose the Cross on her Gown in the High Priestess' Temple

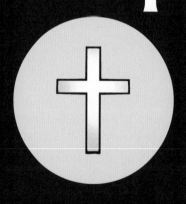

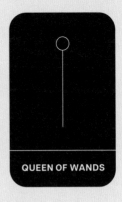

JUDGEMENT   KING OF SWORDS   QUEEN OF WANDS

The question that brought you here: What do I need to know about my life right now?

The hidden knowledge that the Priestess shares with you in a vision is that you are now ready to (re)design your life and future trajectory based on who you authentically are, what you're good at and what you enjoy doing. You and you alone should be, and will be, in control of this process.

Judgement asks you to accept yourself as you are, all the way to the bottom, good and bad, strengths and flaws. Know thyself and know thy opportunity. There is a niche just for you. Strip away comparisons with others, envy and coveting the success you feel you're due. Go back to your authentic nature and build from there.

The King of Swords reveals this is a rational, objective, even intellectual process. Be dispassionate and clear-eyed. Ask for feedback. Create an unvarnished vision of yourself and then decide, like a consultant, what the best use / place / service / value of this person is to the world. That is your niche, your true calling, your home.

When you hit upon the right insight and idea you will just *know* it. The Queen of Wands will emerge from her slumber to inspire you with enthusiasm, vitality and energy to make this vision a reality. Good fortune and opportunity will rise to meet you. Don't worry about the process, it will just magically happen. April, August and December are great months to activate this journey.

You Chose the Crossed Keys in the Hierophant's Sanctum

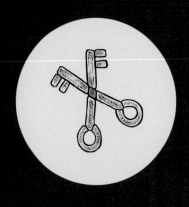

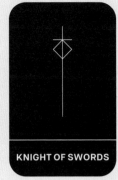

THREE OF COINS   KNIGHT OF SWORDS   STRENGTH

The question that brought you here: What life lesson can I build on right now?

You have come to understand just how deeply admired, respected, liked and loved you are and that your reputation is good. This is worth more than gold. And this knowledge has formed a new bedrock in your self-esteem. The hardships and the way you handled them have gained an unexpected and highly appreciative audience; you set an example, you showed how it's done. Your mettle has inspired others, even if you don't know that. Doing the right thing cements a strong reputation upon which you can build in the future. That is your life lesson.

The Three of Coins reveals the deep and broad admiration you have from other people. Your handling of the trials on your plate have made you someone they'd turn to for advice.

The Knight of Swords shows you found you have reserves of strength, courage and fortitude you didn't know you had until you were tested. Mark Twain said: 'Courage is resistance to fear, mastery of fear, not absence of fear.'

The Strength card unveils the 2.0 version of you that has emerged from all of this – stronger, braver, wiser, kinder, more than you were. The hardships were faced or endured with great dignity and humanity. The example was set. The legacy of this is your sound, revered reputation and position as a person who knows what they're talking about and can be relied upon.

63

You Chose the Crown in the Emperor's Spire

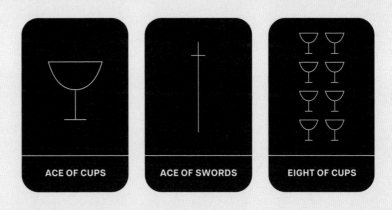

ACE OF CUPS   ACE OF SWORDS   EIGHT OF CUPS

The question that brought you here: What is my next game-changing priority, ambition or goal?

The question that you need to answer to realize your next goal is: 'what would you start next if you knew it couldn't possibly fail?'

The Ace of Cups shows that the objective here is to activate a new passion, a new creative outlet, a magical relationship or collaboration, a 'birth' of some kind. This is heartfelt and warming. This is inspiring and authentically you. This comes from a tentative hope and just needs self-belief and confidence to fuel its activation. Right now is the time.

The Ace of Swords reveals that your guiding light or principle is to be truthful – to yourself and with others. This is about being your authentic self and doing what you truly, deep-down wish to do with your life. No false modesty, shape shifting, or bending to another's will. Follow your own path. Be totally honest with those around you. And, as you tread this path, be honest with yourself too.

The Eight of Cups confirms that your reward is genuine pleasure and fulfilment, after what might feel like a series of disappointments, false starts or dead ends. This is the happy-ever-after you truly desire and it will make all other previous encounters, projects or roles pale into insignificance. They were just preparation for this. You have found your real deal.

65

You Chose the Crystal Walls in the Hermit's Cave

TWO OF WANDS

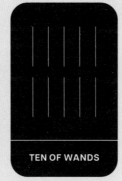
TEN OF WANDS

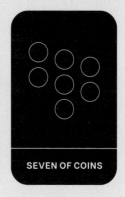
SEVEN OF COINS

The question that brought you here: What do I need to understand about myself?

The nature of the knowledge or enlightenment you seek is the Two of Wands. What is the one single thing, the most important priority, the foundation stone that you need to put above everything else to make your life work and find fulfilment? You have lots of plates spinning, lots of options, lots of stuff you've invested in, begun and feel committed to ... but it lacks structure, priority, focus. Maybe there's too much going on. Maybe you haven't figured out the pecking order. You need to.

The pathway to finding this knowledge is the Ten of Wands. You need deep rest and relaxation, a total mental vacation from this worry or spiral. Seek distraction, rest, play, fun and imaginative, passive pastimes. Seek to soothe and comfort your mind and unwind your body. When you're rested, ideas will flow. Pay passive attention to the 'rocks', or obstacles, your mind returns to most often or most strongly.

The outcome of pursuing, clarifying and understanding this knowledge is the Seven of Coins. There will be change ahead in your life, new doorways opening and shifting the grounds beneath your feet. All are opportunities, as long as you know what's important and can merge the opportunities with your priorities. The Seven of Coins reveals that you are evolving a low-key plan for your long-term future, possibly changing course, and you need a lighter, tighter load on your back to make that change.

You Chose the Daisy in the Fool's Threshold

THE WORLD

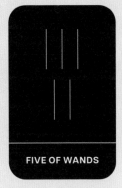
FIVE OF WANDS

FIVE OF CUPS

The question that brought you here: What new beginning am I destined to initiate now?

The nature of your fresh start is revealed by The World. This is a life-changing new beginning which also marks the end of an era. You are changing the story, leaving something behind to pursue a new goal. Location change, travel, house moves, broader territories or scope overseas are all in play. The World is literally about seeing more and using more of this amazing planet.

The outcome or goal of this journey is shared by the Five of Wands. New scene equals new opportunity. Everything about you has the potential to change alongside this shift in location or horizon. There will be a major halo effect and transformation trigger across your wider life, in a good way. Sometimes a different environment completely refreshes our own personality and outlook.

Your first step is introduced by the Five of Cups. Start by thinking what you're ready to move on from. Only then, consider what regrets you do *not* want to carry into your future. Project yourself ahead five, ten, twenty years and imagine the things you don't want to wish you'd got around to, visited, seen, tried or done. Somewhere between leaving something behind and pursuing something new lies the first step of this life transformation.

You Chose
the Dog
in the Fool's
Threshold

THE DEVIL · STRENGTH · SEVEN OF COINS

The question that brought you here: What new beginning am I destined to initiate now?

The nature of your fresh start is revealed by The Devil. You are going to break a habit, release yourself from a long-held pattern, behaviour or self-limiting belief. Freedom and liberation are close by. Once you have replaced this burden with something positive, healthy and inspiring, your life will literally take off. This has been a heavy weight on your back, holding you down. It's time to unveil the 2.0 version of you!

The outcome or goal of this journey is shared by Strength. Massive self-confidence and self-esteem boosts. Massive personal development and growth. This is a major turning point in your life story, making way for a better you, and all you have to do is to release the old habit, replace it with better, and move on. The results will flow in immediately.

Your first step is introduced by the Seven of Coins. Prepare for success. This is a big change and will alter your trajectory going forward. Plan for it. Know yourself, your triggers, your weak spots, your bonds to this habit so that you can break and replace them. Substitution is important. Distraction too. And, of course, rewards! In 28 days' time, you could be free.

You Chose
the Eagle
on the Wheel
of Fortune

72

KING OF CUPS **THREE OF COINS** **PAGE OF SWORDS**

The question that brought you here: What changes lie ahead for me?

The first thing that will change is the King of Cups. An emotional intelligence is brewing, a new perspective, a wiser and shrewder outlook that enables you to process your current situation in a more 'big-picture' way and figure out what needs to happen, what you're responsible for, and what lies outside of your influence. You can only control your own sphere of impact, so focus your energies there and be compassionate and adaptable to everything outside it.

The purpose of this transformation is the Three of Coins: respect, admiration, good reputation. Expect new opportunities and openings in life which come about through your connection with other people. It's who versus what you know. Network and make sure you are visible to people who can bring positive influence and good energy into your life. Look out for people who are born under the Earth signs along this journey: Capricorn, Taurus, Virgo. Look out for people with power and impact, and make sure you're seen by them.

The outcome of this process of change is the Page of Swords. Whole-hearted pursuit of an endeavour you've long wondered about but hesitated to fully commit to. You are setting the wheels in motion that will bring about a 'green light' to go after it with 100% gusto. No more doubts, self-recriminations or half-baked plans. You are all in. It feels great. This pathway is the right one and is leading you towards rewards and joy.

You Chose the Entwined Rose and Lily in the Hierophant's Sanctum

THE MOON   TWO OF SWORDS   THE HIEROPHANT

The question that brought you here: What life lesson can I build on right now?

The knowledge you gained during this hardship has led you to challenge authority and make a different decision in life than you were expected to make. People are surprised, maybe disappointed, but you are happy to disappoint them because you have taken back your power and control – they didn't deserve it. Your life lesson is to always seek the truth, even the hard truth, and to use it. Never suppress, ignore, gloss over or taint it. Work with the truth and you can rebuild from anywhere.

The Moon shows the information you received came initially from a gut feeling or hunch which you followed through. A mystery, illusion or secret was revealed.

The Two of Swords shows you then made a decision and, in hindsight, it's one you could – maybe should – have made sooner but you didn't know then what you know now. Intuition and hunches got the ball rolling but you needed the facts to back them up.

The Hierophant shows this whole episode has a streak of rebellion to it and you challenged an authority or status quo in your life. People are not always what they seem to be, hiding behind a pretence. You saw through it. You came to the truth and you acted. And, in future, you'd trust your gut more. This is the lesson.

You Chose the Feather in the Fool's Threshold

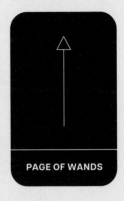

THE HANGED MAN   **THE MAGICIAN**   **PAGE OF WANDS**

The question that brought you here: What new beginning am I destined to initiate now?

The nature of your fresh start is revealed by The Hanged Man. You are going to finally unblock a blockage that has held you back or down for a long, long time. You are aware of this obstacle or restraint and have tried, many times, to overcome it. The trick is going to be to see it all from a new angle, a different perspective, an outside-in viewpoint. Change your mind and change your life.

The outcome or goal of this journey is shared by The Magician. You will create or invent something amazing which has the potential to change your prospects forever! The end game here is about doing what you were born to do, creating the thing that only you can see how to do. You are going to finally access and utilize that deep well of imagination and ability within.

Your first step is introduced by the Page of Wands. Experimentation! You need to start trying different approaches, thinking out of the box, getting the off-the-wall and unusual opinions and perspectives and really using them. The way ahead is found through trial and error. There are no wrong steps; everything has value and contributes to this wild ride in some way. No regrets, just set off!

You Chose the Flowers in The Magician's Chamber

SEVEN OF CUPS   **ACE OF COINS**   **KING OF SWORDS**

The question that brought you here: What is my unique talent or power in this lifetime?

Your hidden power is to cultivate and fulfil the potential in people, to heal, teach, inspire, as shown by Seven of Cups and Ace of Coins. This isn't about teaching because you can't do it yourself, this is about authentic inspiration – touching the lives of others in ways you can't fathom right now. This isn't a direct A to B route; this is curling and complex.

The Ace of Coins gifts you materially with a 'Midas touch'. You won't struggle because what you do is needed by so many, what you give is what others want, you are in demand. And the good you bring to the world racks up the 'good karma credit' in the Universe's accounts, bringing you many happy surprises and opportunities.

The King of Swords shows that you will reach your full potential with this skill later on in life when you have your own experiences and wisdom to share. This is a mature pathway, a gift that increasingly unfolds the more fully you live your life. So, enjoy it all! Seek creativity, inspiration, education, learning and information. Experience everything. Absorb as much as you can.

You will benefit by focusing on and practising your creative talents, finding outlets and the means to express yourself which could become tangible products you can share with the wider world.

You can bond easily and effortlessly with all the zodiac signs. You are a universal networker and connector.

79

You Chose the Hanging Globe in the Emperor's Spire

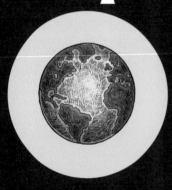

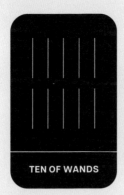
TEN OF WANDS

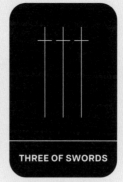
THREE OF SWORDS

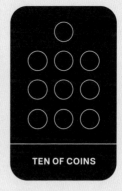
TEN OF COINS

The question that brought you here: What is my next game-changing priority, ambition or goal?

The question that you need to answer to realize your next goal is 'what is the most comfortable and natural happy-ever-after daydream I think about?'

The Ten of Wands shows that the objective here is to reach an understanding of your default 'happy place' – what you naturally, and without force or effort, love doing and flows easily with you. Where do you drift to in your head when you're thinking of happy things? Who were you with? Where were you? What were you doing?

The Three of Swords reveals that your guiding light or principle here is to strip away the bad stuff – the force, pain, toxicity, poison, effort without reward, and dead weight. We start life unencumbered and free and, as we walk our paths, things mount up on our backs. Lighten this load. Put down what doesn't serve or nourish you. Once it's all gone, you will see more clearly what your dream destination or life really is about.

The Ten of Coins confirms that your reward is the happy-ever-after you dream about; you are destined to reach this place and make this dream a reality. You are going to create a beautiful life, you will find everything you need, and make intuitive decisions along the way. It starts with a vision. Let yourself dream.

You Chose the Heart Brooch in the Empress' Paradise

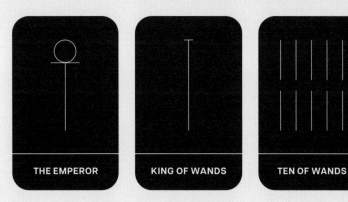

THE EMPEROR **KING OF WANDS** **TEN OF WANDS**

The question that brought you here: How will I meet my next love?

The person on the cards for you is The Emperor. Likely an Aries, this is a strong, powerful, somewhat dominant, ambitious, go-getting, successful, driven individual who makes an impact wherever they go. They are confident, in control and fixated on getting ahead, doing better, building an empire. You might find yourself having to fight at times to make sure the power dynamics between you are balanced, but that's okay. This person makes a huge difference to your life.

You will meet them through the King of Wands. The months of April, August and December look positive. A Fire-sign friend – Aries, Leo or Sagittarius – or contact could introduce you. The theme of adventure is strong here, an outing, trip, event or venue which is linked to thrills and challenges (sports, theme park, gym, scarey maze!). You are already excited to be at this place and then you meet this dynamic person.

The one step you can take *today* to move closer to this love is shown by the Ten of Wands. Stop looking! Seriously, you know how they say that things happen when you're not looking, well the Ten of Wands is saying just that. Rest, relax, please yourself, do stuff that you enjoy, be around good people ... do all of that and love will arrive.

You Chose the Horned Moon Diadem Crown in the High Priestess' Temple

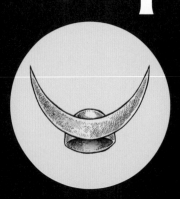

SEVEN OF COINS

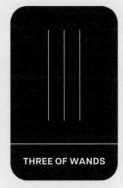

THREE OF WANDS

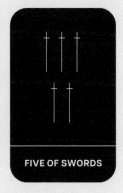

FIVE OF SWORDS

The question that brought you here: What do I need to know about my life right now?

The hidden knowledge that the Priestess shares with you in a vision is that the opportunities you seize, act on, and make the most of in a positive sense will plant the seeds that you reap for the coming decade. This is planting season – be shrewd, be hopeful, be confident.

The Seven of Coins reveals a new seven- to ten-year chapter is stretching out ahead of you and the embryo of it is in your hands, in your gift, right now. The opportunities you take, the moves you make, the priorities you focus on, and the good habits or behaviours you adopt will all work to affect the potential and outcome of this chapter.

There are more opportunities around you than you realize. You should adjust your perception, perhaps to be broader, more open-minded and welcoming, more attuned to the left-field and unexpected or random. The Three of Wands shows that many of these opportunities are fast-moving, so you need to adopt a gut-feeling kind of response mechanism. Don't overthink things.

Most importantly, seek peace, seek resolutions, seek to compromise and agree on ways forward with those you've quarrelled or struggled with. Even if the decision is to agree to disagree and part ways, that in itself is still a peaceful outcome. Leave all grudges and tension and conflict behind now. The Five of Swords shows there's no place for any of that in your glowing future chapter. Bury it.

You Chose the Infinity Symbol in The Magician's Chamber

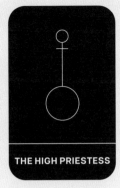
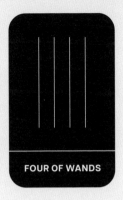

KNIGHT OF CUPS **THE HIGH PRIESTESS** **FOUR OF WANDS**

The question that brought you here: What is my unique talent or power in this lifetime?

Your hidden power is psychic ability and intuition, as shown by The High Priestess. You possess deep, limitless and accurate resources of knowledge, awareness, instinct and understanding. This well will never run dry nor fail you. Trust your intuition, learn to lean on it and use it as a sat nav to guide you. Know, and believe, that you will always be able to find answers.

Helping others and guiding, counselling, advising, healing and supporting them is the likely best use of this powerful gift, as shown by the compassionate, inspiring and helpful Knight of Cups. You can lift people. You understand them and their true motivation, desire and experience. You can change the atmosphere of a room and charge it with positivity.

The Four of Wands shows that you will reach your full potential with this skill relatively soon, it is *all* already there, you just need to trust yourself to lean on it. A step up in responsibility or role may activate it fully.

You can aim as high as you wish to in the fields related to this skill – psychology, medicine, teaching, the arts, spirituality and the esoteric.

Look for Water-sign people (Scorpio, Cancer or Pisces) to provide you with a sounding board, a place you can put your own troubles down and rest easy. You need support too.

You Chose the Kneeling Monks in the Hierophant's Sanctum

FOUR OF WANDS　　**KING OF WANDS**　　**PAGE OF CUPS**

The question that brought you here: What life lesson can I build on right now?

Taking a chance and acting on instinct pays off, eventually, even if there are a few wrong turns or stumbles along the way. You have risen because you took risks, played a bold hand, acted on your gut, and somehow kept a strong thread back to your childhood self, back to your roots, your authentic inner passions or interests. When you follow your authentic desires – even if the path is winding and shadowed – you will reach the light! Your life lesson is to always follow your heart, pursue a passion, do what makes you feel excited and hopeful, even when others disapprove.

The Four of Wands reveals your progress, your rise, your success. You recognized what you were good at, enjoyed or made you tick and you followed it up and through, riding a wave.

The King of Wands applauds your confidence, luck, tenacity, self-belief and persistence. You kept going when others would have fallen by the wayside; you backed yourself, you took chances. Fortune favours the bold.

The Page of Cups underpins this story with a nod to your childhood or a younger version of you, to whom you owe some of this. There is an inner child in all of us, and you listened to and understood yours, and gave them the chance to get what they wanted, after all this time.

You Chose the Lantern in the Hermit's Cave

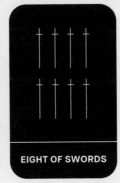

WHEEL OF FORTUNE　**EIGHT OF SWORDS**　**THE LOVERS**

The question that brought you here: What do I need to understand about myself?

The nature of the knowledge or enlightenment you seek is the Wheel of Fortune. You want change but you don't know exactly what, how, or where to begin. Everything feels foggy, confusing, ambiguous so you feel lost, struggling, unclear ... but still holding onto a deep-seated belief that change is what is needed. You just need to find and focus on the first step: the glimmer of light ahead that guides you towards the fresh start or new beginning you need to activate. Everything will flow from there. You don't need the whole story, just the opening line. Focus on that.

The pathway to finding this knowledge is the Eight of Swords. Get out of your own way. Appreciate that much of the fog is your own projection and self-made illusion. You project your fears externally as barriers to keep you in place, to limit yourself, to keep you safe with The Devil you know best.

The outcome of pursuing, clarifying and understanding this knowledge is The Lovers: clarity at last, a foundation on which to build. The gift of certainty, even if only the first step, will unlock a new chapter for you and help you to ignite a series of changes which will cast a positive halo effect across your whole life. All you need is that first step, that opening line, that glimmer of light.

You Chose the Lion on the Wheel of Fortune

THE MAGICIAN   **THE LOVERS**   **THE HANGED MAN**

The question that brought you here: What changes lie ahead for me?

The first thing that will change is The Magician. You are brimming with creativity and imaginative ideas. You have recognized your own talents and strengths and are taking responsibility for using them, bringing them to the foreground. Why waste what is naturally yours to utilise? Why not make a living doing what you're good at, enjoy, and find easy? You are powerful and you are beginning to truly believe it! This realization is at the heart of this life shift.

The purpose of this transformation is The Lovers. You are being nudged towards a life pathway fuelled by passion and heartfelt desire. You want to be in love with what you do. You want to create and innovate. You want to be the star of the show, the creator, the master, the driver of the engine. You are tired of wondering 'what if' and feel like it's time to find out! There's nothing to lose. Test yourself, put your ideas in motion, find out the way by doing and trying instead of overthinking.

The outcome of this process of change is The Hanged Man. The stalled, limbo situation you have found yourself drawn into recently will lift completely and momentum will gather and build fast. Everything will accelerate. The halo effect of this change will be life-wide! You won't be the same person this time next year, you will feel more fulfilled and rewarded and inspired than ever. When you take on this challenge, you *will* rise to the occasion and discover new depths to your creativity and power. A new outlook is emerging.

93

You Chose the Lunar Crescent in the High Priestess' Temple

PAGE OF SWORDS

FOUR OF CUPS

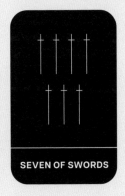

SEVEN OF SWORDS

The question that brought you here: What do I need to know about my life right now?

The hidden knowledge that the Priestess shares with you in a vision is that there are people or situations in your life which are poisoning your mood and energies. You need a clear-out and a revamp of your relationship landscape and roles.

The Seven of Swords and Four of Cups combine to reveal this process will begin this week and, within seven months, you will end up feeling totally refreshed, energized and full of life again. You don't realize the drag and weight these insidious forces have exerted upon you (and you won't fully realize it until you are free of it). People are not all as wholesome and well-meaning as you are. Some roles are just no longer serving you. Some situations will never be resolved and it's best to part ways peacefully and start anew. Recognize the dead wood and dead weight.

The Page of Swords shows that you have felt this way for a while but have tried to carry on regardless, being all things to all people, and doing your duties without complaint. You have given benefits of the doubt, ignored red flags, battled to reconcile your expectations. Enough of this mental gymnastics and shape-shifting! Liberate yourself from the things that don't fit, suit or serve you. Be decisive and stoic in this process. Don't seek trouble or conflict. Just seek exits and retreats and clearance. New opportunity and energy will flow in to replace everything that you cut away.

95

You Chose the Mountain Pool in the Hermit's Cave

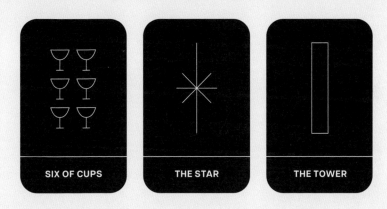

SIX OF CUPS   THE STAR   THE TOWER

The question that brought you here: What do I need to understand about myself?

The nature of the knowledge or enlightenment you seek is the Six of Cups. Nostalgia, the past, your childhood, your original / authentic self without the tarnishes or pressures of adulthood and outside commitments. What did you truly love doing, were good at, praised for, and found easy or natural? We often spend our adult lives searching for our niche only to find it was what we did so well and easily as children. Look deep into the mountain pool and retrace your steps. Visit 'Memory Lane'. Reconnect with your past.

The pathway to finding this knowledge is The Star. Make a wish. Have a hope. Dare to dream. Trust that the Universe is going to grant you what you wish for and bring you good fortune and opportunity. Your job is simply to define that wish. And that wish is linked to finding your niche in this life based on what you were born to do, what your childhood self always intuitively understood to be your gift.

The outcome of pursuing, clarifying and understanding this knowledge is The Tower. Be ready to accept that your true pathway, purpose and destiny may lie outside what you're currently doing. Perhaps you will need to dismantle a current way of life or of earning a living in order to rebuild this new, more you-suited world. Be ready to pivot.

You Chose the Pearl Necklace in the Empress' Paradise

TEN OF CUPS   **NINE OF CUPS**   **THE CHARIOT**

The question that brought you here: How will I meet my next love?

The person on the cards for you is the Ten of Cups, who is likely to be a Water sign (Pisces, Cancer or Scorpio). This is a dream lover, a vision of love, an ideal version of your perfect partner. The attraction is strong, immediate and passionate. This feels like falling in love at first sight, like a movie romance. It's epic.

You will meet them through the Nine of Cups: manifesting, making a wish, truly believing and using the Law of Attraction. Nine of Cups is a dream-come-true card, a 'wish pass' from the Universe granting you a heart's desire. This love is just around the corner; a matter of days (weeks at most). The months of March, July and November also look positive.

The one step you can take *today* to move closer to this love is shown by The Chariot. Travel, explore, take a new route, visit the venue that just opened, book a holiday, take a different mode of transport. See more of the world in a new way, in whatever way is feasible for you in the coming two weeks! This new territory is where this love is. A new scene means a new opportunity.

You Chose the Pentacle in the Devil's Underworld

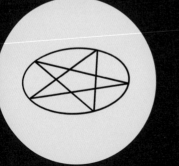

SIX OF WANDS

THE MOON

SIX OF CUPS

The question that brought you here: What message does my shadow self yearn to reveal to me?

Your shadow self's origin is Six of Wands. This shadow self cannot bear to face bad news, deal with unexpected setbacks or issues, or recognize when something is negative, even toxic. This shadow self possesses enormous powers of imagination and creativity to create excuses, reasons and plausible justifications for things which are, truthfully, downright wrong and need exorcizing from your realm. This shadow self makes you linger for too long in situations that are not good for you.

It is triggered by The Moon. When there is doubt or concern or unanswered questions swirling around you, this self awakens and paints a gloss over everything to stop you looking too closely and getting hurt by a hard truth. It creates illusions to keep you happy. Alas, they work too well and actually you only end up being hurt later on anyway. It's time to dispel these illusions and deceits.

You can bring peace and healing to your shadow self with the Six of Cups: deep affection and love, self-care and self-respect. Protect yourself well and treat yourself like the treasured inner child you still are! How you treat yourself teaches others how to treat you, too, and when your shadow self realizes how precious you are, it will stop trying to keep you in negative situations.

You Chose the Ram-adorned Throne in the Emperor's Spire

THE MOON

QUEEN OF SWORDS

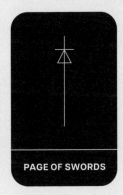
PAGE OF SWORDS

The question that brought you here: What is my next game-changing priority, ambition or goal?

The question that you need to answer to realize your next goal is 'what is the greatest unsolved mystery, secret or mystical energy in your life?'

The Moon shows that the objective here is to solve the case, crack the code, get to the bottom of things, know the unknown, answer the question, or bring clarity to confusion. The Moon shows this mystery holds important power and knowledge within its realm and, once entered, your pathway will be illuminated. You need this knowledge.

The Queen of Swords reveals that your guiding light or principle is to do this alone, by yourself, intellectually, dispassionately. Create a strategy, a series of tactics, a schedule. Execute it, review results, create the next strategy, tactics, schedule and go again. Keep going. Research your way to an answer that feels new, right, intuitive, and highlights your next step.

The Page of Swords confirms that your reward is clarity, surety, stability, answers. When you have the right foundation of understanding, you will know what you need to do next; it will be obvious. Knowledge is power. Knowledge provides you with options and ideas, all possible pathways unfold when you have information. Knowledge will illuminate your next big goal in life.

103

You Chose the Ring in the Devil's Underworld

SEVEN OF CUPS

TWO OF SWORDS

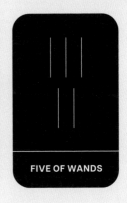

FIVE OF WANDS

The question that brought you here: What message does my shadow self yearn to reveal to me?

Your shadow self's origin is Seven of Cups. An over-active imagination, an ability to visualize and create a dream of what might be, of what could unfold, of what if ... This has the positive of enabling you to be creative and imaginative, and you've been like that since childhood, but it does bring you bad dreams and catastrophized spiralling thoughts, too. You control your mind, but sometimes it doesn't feel that way.

It is triggered by the Two of Swords. Decision-making and choices are the ignition point for this shadow self to emerge and bring you scary visions of what could happen if you get it 'wrong'. This can lead to procrastination and overthinking which, in turn, can lead to missed opportunities and outcomes because you feel paralysed by the worst case scenarios that your shadow self tortures you with.

You can bring peace and healing to your shadow self with the Five of Wands. Force it to walk beside you on time-constrained challenges and short-term decisions, so it can understand that nothing is irreversible or a lost cause. The worst decision can be rectified. New decisions can be made every day. No situation remains static. Things change quickly. Show your shadow self that nothing is set in stone, and there's a new opportunity to start anew every day.

You Chose the Sceptre in the Hierophant's Sanctum

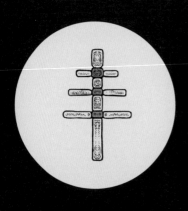

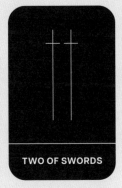

THE MOON **TWO OF SWORDS** **THE HIEROPHANT**

The question that brought you here: What life lesson can I build on right now?

The knowledge you gained during this particular hardship has led you to challenge authority and make a different decision in life than you were expected to make. People are surprised, perhaps disappointed, but you are happy to disappoint them because you have taken back your power and control – they didn't deserve it. Your life lesson is to always seek the truth, even the hard truth, and to use it. Never suppress, ignore, gloss over or taint it. Work with the truth and you can rebuild from anywhere.

The Moon shows the information you received came initially from a gut feeling or hunch that you followed through. A mystery, illusion or secret was revealed.

The Two of Swords shows you then made a decision and, in hindsight, it's one you could (or maybe should) have made sooner but you didn't know then what you know now. Intuition and hunches got the ball rolling but you needed the facts, too.

The Hierophant shows this whole episode has a streak of rebellion to it and you challenged an authority or status quo in your life. People are not always what they seem to be, hiding behind a pretence. You saw through it. You came to the truth and you acted. And, in future, you'll trust your gut more. This is the lesson.

107

You Chose the Scroll in the High Priestess' Temple

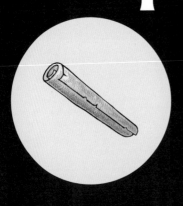

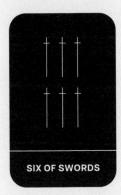
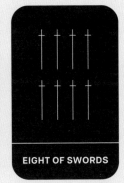
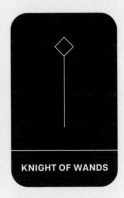

SIX OF SWORDS   EIGHT OF SWORDS   KNIGHT OF WANDS

The question that brought you here: What life lesson can I build on right now?

The hidden knowledge that the Priestess shares with you in a vision is that you are shedding an old self and will make departures and exits in your life as you recognize you have outgrown your old spaces, places and aspirations. The 2.0 version of you is coming.

The Six of Swords reveals that you will be making these moves in the coming six to eight months, with particular emphasis on the months of February, June and October overall in this transformation process.

The Eight of Swords show that you begin the transformation by seeing clearly, with absolute clarity and self-awareness, the ways in which you get in your own way, undermine yourself, talk yourself down or out. You notice you project your inner fears outside onto the world or other people as barrier which, hold you in position. You realize you have been in a loop, a pattern, a series of habits borne out of fear or insecurity. This knowledge is liberating, freeing, empowering. You can control yourself, so therefore you can change this spiral.

The Knight of Wands asks you to go on an adventure, a series of challenges designed to target these fears, make you face them, overcome them, and finally bury them in the past behind you. Travel, education, creativity and new lifestyle routines or rituals are all welcome right now. Change your mind, change your life, change your future.

You Chose the Serpent Statue in the Magician's Chamber

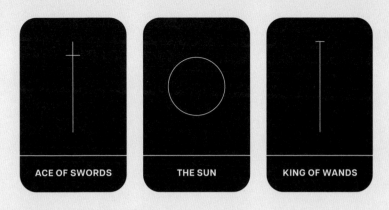

ACE OF SWORDS · THE SUN · KING OF WANDS

The question that brought you here: What is my unique talent or power in this lifetime?

Your hidden power is truth (which becomes wisdom as you mature), as shown by the Ace of Swords. You are not fazed, awed, intimidated or confused by truth and see things with crystal clarity – the good, bad and ugly. The gifts don't stop there, though, because The Sun is the tarot's most positive card and reveals you also know how to 'land' truths in a way that means they are received well, understood, taken to heart and acted upon. This makes you a catalyst and a provocative, progressive influence.

Activism, campaigning, teaching, writing, journalism, research, broadcasting, presenting. You like to speak up, express yourself, share your truths, see how they persuade and change people's minds.

The King of Wands reveals you may find a mentor along the way who really helps you to understand the rawness of your power of truth-seeing and how to harness it. Put yourself around older, wiser, more empathetic people and listen deeply to their stories, guidance and wisdom. Surround yourself with sage and perceptive people.

Look for Fire sign people (Leo, Aries, Sagittarius) to be allies and friends as you journey through life. You can feed from their energy, positivity and power as you make your stand, share your ideas and change the world!

111

You Chose the Sheaf of Wheat in the Empress' Paradise

PAGE OF COINS   **THE HANGED MAN**   **EIGHT OF CUPS**

The question that brought you here: How will I meet my next love?

The person on the cards for you is the Page of Coins. Likely an Earth sign (Capricorn, Virgo or Taurus) and possibly slightly younger or in some kind of student / apprentice phase of their life. This person is ambitious, going places, and eager to learn and improve. They are loyal, stoic, steadfast, worldly and ready for a committed union and to create a beautiful life with someone equally ambitious.

You will meet them through The Hanged Man. The key here is to escape, overcome or demolish a current situation in your life that is holding you in limbo. Something is thwarting your progress and growth and your experience of life. Something has stalled and is frustrating you. Look at it from all angles and different perspectives until you experience that 'aha!' moment that unlocks your escape. It is during this escape you will meet this Page.

The one step you can take today to move closer to this love is shown by the Eight of Cups. Accept your disappointments and release them. Don't make excuses or suppress or cover up a situation that isn't working out ... face it, end it, withdraw from it. The sooner you do, the sooner this new person will find you and you can escape your limbo. A new chapter is dawning.

You Chose
the Snake
on the Wheel
of Fortune

DEATH   SIX OF CUPS   KING OF CUPS

The question that brought you here: What changes lie ahead for me?

The first thing that will change is Death. A major life event, probably outside of your control or influence (an unseen force) which shakes up your grounding, outlook, priorities and ideas about what could come next. This catalyst is deep-rooted and necessary. It comes to herald a total change of heart and mind about your future. Embrace it. Work with it.

The purpose of this transformation is the Six of Cups. The past matters. There is something, someplace, or someone that you still feel great connection to and affection for, and it's time to rekindle and reinvent that relationship. Perhaps it is a literal relationship, perhaps a location or role you once loved, perhaps an activity, talent or strength that you enjoyed in your childhood or youth. Sometimes we need to look back in order to move forward.

The outcome of this process of change is the King of Cups: growth, stability, peace, love, joy, emotional balance and security, wisdom, satisfaction, reward and success! You need to feel 'in love', whether that is with who you're with, where you are, or what you do, and that is the yardstick to measure your current position against. What have you lost that you once loved? Perhaps you need to reinvent and return to it.

You Chose the Sphinx on the Wheel of Fortune

QUEEN OF SWORDS   KNIGHT OF COINS   EIGHT OF CUPS

The question that brought you here: What changes lie ahead for me?

The first thing that will change is the Queen of Swords: self-awareness, self-reliance, self-importance. You are starting to see that if you don't take control and shape your destiny, you'll be at the mercy of others' designs. The Queen of Swords is your new attitude – sharp, direct, ruthless, self-centred, powerful, intelligent and cerebral. You are thinking more clearly and more quickly than ever. Your ideas feel charged with energy and purpose.

The purpose of this transformation is the Knight of Coins: security, legacy, material gain, wealth, recognition, protection. You want to create your own empire, your own source of surety and reward. You are going to put everything into this and the rewards will equal that effort so work hard, work harder than you've ever worked. Look out for Earth signs along this journey (Capricorn, Taurus or Virgo). Look out for people with power and impact, and make sure you're seen by them.

The outcome of this process of change is the Eight of Cups. Somewhere along the way, this project, relationship or endeavour will shift and you might think you made the wrong commitment or decision. You didn't. There's a bump in the road but it serves only to nudge you onto the right track and you can't get there without first taking *this* path. Don't be put off, disgruntled, discouraged or frustrated by issues. Use them, adapt to them, change as a result of them. The best is all to come.

117

You Chose the Staff in The Hermit's Cave

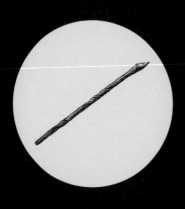

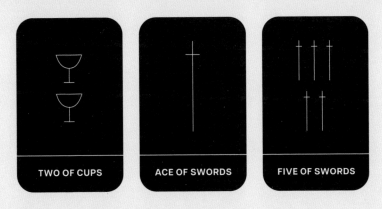

TWO OF CUPS　　**ACE OF SWORDS**　　**FIVE OF SWORDS**

The question that brought you here: What do I need to understand about myself?

The nature of the knowledge or enlightenment you seek is the Two of Cups: relationship wisdom. You need knowledge and insight about the person who is most important to you right now and with whom you are trying to forge a mutually beneficial, close and supportive bond for the future. You wish to lean on them and have them know they can lean on you. This might be a romantic love, but it could also be with a family member, close friend, ally, or even creative / career partner.

The pathway to finding this knowledge is the Ace of Swords. All strong relationships are forged in truth, authenticity and reality. No illusions, games, lies or secrets. Getting to know each deeply and more intimately is the pathway to true alignment and trust.

The outcome of pursuing, clarifying and understanding this knowledge is the Five of Swords. There is likely to be a burning phase, a trial, a period of conflict or misunderstanding or tension. Ride it out. New information can change things, feel bruising, undermine hopes or ideals you were holding onto. Let that all go. Ride the waves. Find the truth and re-forge an honest and authentic understanding so that you can lean on each other, trust each other, and know each other.

You Chose the Swords in the Emperor's Spire

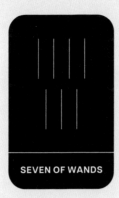
SEVEN OF WANDS

THE EMPRESS

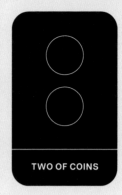
TWO OF COINS

The question that brought you here: What is my next game-changing priority, ambition or goal?

The question that you need to answer to realize your next goal is 'what would you fight to have more of in your life?'.

The Seven of Wands shows that the objective here is to test your appetite for fighting, force, protection, defence. What stirs you? What would you go out of your way to get more of or protect what you already have? Perhaps imagine losing certain things or future potential opportunities and assess your body's reactions. Our bodies hold so much intelligence, they know what we feel before our brain kicks into gear.

The Empress reveals that your guiding light or principle is about passion and love. This isn't a protective or fighting instinct nurtured by hate or jealousy or self-doubt. This is activated by a deep love, pride, desire, thirst. You want this; you must have it. The Empress can represent love, sex, passion, pregnancy, family, home, creativity, nesting.

The Two of Coins confirms that your reward is abundance. Focus on what you desire. Make sure this is what you want! You are about to flood your life with your heart's desire. There is no limit to what you can attract into your world with the right beacon, or frequency, ignited within.

You Chose the Three-tiered Crown in the Hierophant's Sanctum

THE MOON   TWO OF SWORDS   THE HIEROPHANT

The question that brought you here: What life lesson can I build on right now?

The knowledge you gained through hardships in your life has led you to challenge authority and make a different decision in life than you were expected to make. People are surprised, perhaps disappointed, but you are happy to disappoint them because you have taken back your power and control – they didn't deserve it. Your life lesson is to always seek the truth, even the hard truth, and to use it. Never suppress, ignore, gloss over or taint it. Work with the truth and you can rebuild from anywhere.

The Moon shows the information you received came initially from a gut feeling or hunch which you followed through. A mystery, illusion or secret was revealed.

The Two of Swords shows you then made a decision and, in hindsight, it's one you could – and perhaps should – have made sooner, but you didn't know then what you know now. Intuition and hunches got the ball rolling but you needed the facts too.

The Hierophant shows this whole episode has a streak of rebellion to it and you challenged an authority or status quo in your life. People are not always what they seem to be, hiding behind a pretence. You saw through it. You came to learn the truth and you acted. And, in future, you'll trust your gut more. This is the lesson.

123

You Chose
the Torch
in the Devil's
Underworld

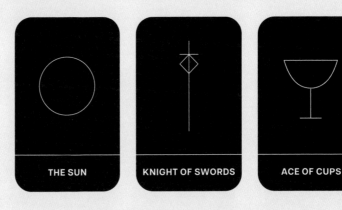

THE SUN   **KNIGHT OF SWORDS**   **ACE OF CUPS**

The question that brought you here: What message does my shadow self yearn to reveal to me?

Your shadow self's origin is The Sun. You have a powerful ego, a strong sense of your self-worth, and you're very passionate and ambitious. These are positive traits but, within them, lurks a shadow version which can tip into arrogance, inflexibility and resistance to change or outside input. You want to be in control and taking the lead. Your shadow self came about to ensure that always happened ... even when, perhaps, it wasn't the best outcome for the situation or relationship overall.

It is triggered by the Knight of Swords. It is the fight part of your fight-or-flight mechanism. When you feel a threat or challenge from someone or something for supremacy or the leadership spot, this shadow self awakens and takes control of the situation. It can be angry, immature, selfish and demanding. This shadow self will do whatever it takes to keep you in prime position.

You can bring peace and healing to your shadow self with the Ace of Cups: a new beginning, a fresh start, a clean slate. Promise it that the real win is the outcome, the end game, the result and that the best outcomes come via positive and mutual collaborations and partnerships. Two heads are better than one. Ask your shadow self to make friends with those it thinks are rivals, to join forces with foes, to work together with others for the goal of greater success for everyone. This is a new era of success and prosperity.

125

You Chose the Veil in The High Priestess' Temple

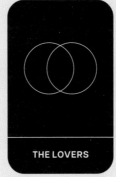
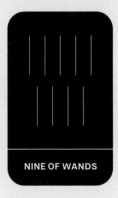

KNIGHT OF SWORDS   **THE LOVERS**   **NINE OF WANDS**

The question that brought you here: What do I need to know about my life right now?

The hidden knowledge that the Priestess shares with you in a vision is that it is time to face and tackle your greatest fear or challenge, the one you've dreaded and always known will emerge one day. Don't live in dread any longer, take action instead. The power you will gain by vanquishing this darkness will be immeasurable. This is a game-changing period of your life.

The Knight of Swords puts you in fighting mode, on the front foot, finding the reserves of strength, courage, resilience and determination to overcome anything in your path. Use this power and force to push through your biggest challenge; you have all you need to achieve your goal.

The Lovers reveals this is an obstacle you feel emotive about, and probably lost sleep along the way wondering about how you'll face it. Stop wondering and start realizing. Summon your power. The Lovers shows that you might feel ambivalent or like distracting yourself with a million other tasks or projects ... don't! Focus.

The Nine of Wands promises this is not going to be half as bad, hard, onerous or testing as you fear. Your dread is mostly vapour and will evaporate as you move from thinking to doing mode. The Universe is backing you up on this endeavour and you will succeed.

You Chose the Wand in the Magician's Chamber

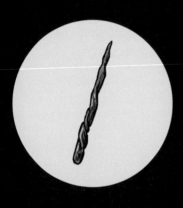

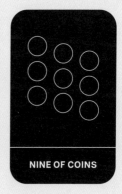

KING OF COINS   **PAGE OF WANDS**   **NINE OF COINS**

The question that brought you here: What is my unique talent or power in this lifetime?

Your hidden power is manifesting better futures, as shown by two strong Coins cards. This is about tangible, practical and positive change which you dream up, visualize and execute and make a reality. You're an empire builder, a game changer, a creator of new realities. The King of Coins shows you working for yourself, being a leader, and weathering every storm, turning challenge to experience, and making yourself wealthy along the way. The Nine of Coins is a road to self-improvement and positive change. You are a visionary of 'what if'.

Fields associated with this pathway could cover technology, architecture, engineering, medicine, business, property development, finance, philanthropy, and charity.

The Page of Wands shows that you will reach your full potential in a relatively chaotic kind of way! There is no overnight sensation or singular decision that brings about this talent's emergence and fulfilment. It comes with experience, trial and error, success and failure You grow your way into this niche. Everything you do along the way is valuable.

Look for Earth-sign people (Capricorn, Virgo, Taurus) to work with you and support your goals, to bring what you may lack or dislike, to fill the gaps, to complement your skill set.

Always look to the future, to the new opportunity, to tomorrow. You will get lots of second, third and fourth chances to succeed. This is a marathon, not a sprint. Keep trying, failing and trying again.

You Chose the Robe in the Magician's Chamber

ACE OF WANDS

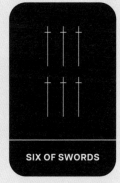

SIX OF SWORDS

KING OF WANDS

The question that brought you here: What is my unique talent or power in this lifetime?

Your hidden power is creativity, as shown by two Wands cards. However, you receive the first and last of the suit so there will be a journey in activating and realizing this power in your life. You will need to consciously focus on it and bring it out with training, education, coaching and practice. This path forms with experience.

Writing is a strong possibility, be that fiction, journalism, poetry, political speech-writing, foreign languages, song-writing or even acting and presenting.

The Six of Swords shows that you will reach your full potential with this skill midway in your life, following a change or departure. Something you leave behind will release the pent-up creative power, motivation and desire to bring out, and work on, this talent.

You will begin a course or project which helps you to develop.

Look for Fire-sign people (Leo, Aries, Sagittarius) to inspire you, either through their example, or encouragement and teaching.

Don't be scared, when the time comes, to make a leap from your current role or position and pursue this full time or with more gusto. The Six of Swords shows that you will end up making a living with this talent, but it will mean a change of direction, a brave move, a bold leap. When that time comes, you will feel ready, willing and capable. It will feel like the right move, even if it still seems risky or sudden.

You Chose the Wreath in the Empress' Paradise

SIX OF CUPS

KING OF CUPS

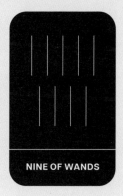
NINE OF WANDS

The question that brought you here: How will I meet my next love?

The person on the cards for you is the Six of Cups. Likely a Water sign (Pisces, Cancer, Scorpio), an affectionate, loving, loyal, warm and playful person who is easy company and has an uplifting, soothing presence. You feel at home with them, as if you've known them all your life. Perhaps they do have a link to your past, maybe someone you once admired or who is from the same town.

You will meet them through the King of Cups. Summer is positive for this love. The months of March, July and November also look positive. It's possible that an older, emotionally intelligent and wise man plays Cupid here, or at least introduces you. Notice people who are overtly kind, giving, charitable, and loved by others. Draw closer to those who seem comforting and joyful.

The one step you can take TODAY to move closer to this love is shown by the Nine of Wands. Swallow your fears and face your dread. Do the things you know you need to do but which scare or worry you. Face them and deal with them. The Nine of Wands promises you can do it, things won't be as bad as you think, and this love is linked to this process of overcoming challenge. Grow, learn, thrive.

133

You Chose the Zodiac Crown in the Empress' Paradise

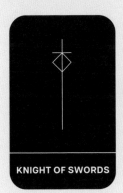

KNIGHT OF SWORDS

THE MAGICIAN

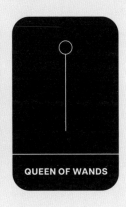

QUEEN OF WANDS

The question that brought you here: How will I meet my next love?

The person on the cards for you is the Knight of Swords. Most likely an Air sign (Gemini, Libra, Aquarius), a strong, sparky, challenging character who knows their own mind, is bold and ambitious, and will fight for you and your love. They are someone who keeps you on your toes and you enjoy verbally sparring with them. When they support you, you feel unstoppable; they are a wonderful ally in life.

You will meet them through The Magician. The months of June and September look positive. A Gemini or Virgo friend or contact could introduce you, or maybe a meeting will come about via a place of education and learning or creativity. Seek classes, forums, workshops, lectures, events and exhibitions which look enlivening and interesting.

The one step you can take *today* to move closer to this love is shown by the Queen of Wands. Step up and book something NEW in your life which links to either education, creativity, travel or lifestyle rituals and routines (exercise, hobbies, groups). Take ownership for this, seek and research options, choose the thing which lifts your spirits, inspires you, and feels like a new adventure.

Moving
Forward

I hope this book has intrigued, inspired and interested you in learning more about tarot and perhaps trying to use the cards yourself.

Of course, you can always just stick with this book and return to your guides as and when you feel you need to receive a message. They will always be here for you, waiting for your attention, hoping to provide their guidance, helping you to figure out your destiny, and wishing you well on your journey through life.

Happy travels.

Acknowledgements

Thank you to Kate Pollard and Hardie Grant, for taking on this unique idea of tarot reading. I know it's a risk; I know it's new and different. Kate, bless you for spinning the wheel of fortune! A big thank you to Magdalena Kaczan, for bringing this book to living, breathing, vibrant life – the illustrations have surpassed my wildest dreams. Thank you to Wendy Hobson, for always making my words way better, way, way better. You are a genius. And thank you so much to Claire Warner, who has taken this concept and made it look uber cool and contemporary. I am thrilled with it, thank you deeply.

Thank you to 'childhood me', for having such a wide and weird scope of reading material. Take it from me, NOTHING you experience or take on is wasted. Everything goes into the melting pot of your psyche and mixes and matches with what else is there. The more stimulus you absorb, the more opportunities for unique amalgamations you will be exposed to. Cheers to the magical writings of Ian Livingstone and Steven Jackson and their 'Fighting Fantasy' series – it activated this idea for sure.

I always have one eye beyond the veil. I feel my allies on the other side every day, willing me on, and I know you're there rooting for me. We will meet again: Dad, Brodie, Winnie, Minnie, Geoff, Barbara, Rita, Audrey. I will join you and celebrate with you, hopefully for a life well lived.

Thank you to my kind, selfless, patient mother, Freda. Although we are very different, you have always let me be me, and let me do all my weird stuff without interference or rebuke.

A deep thank you to all of my lovely family, fabulous friendship circle, and co-pilot through life, Luke. Without your presence, love, support and humour, I couldn't do what I do. And I know it.

About the Author

Kerry Ward is a tarot reader, deck creator, writer and *Cosmopolitan* US and UK's first resident tarot columnist. Kerry has been reading tarot for over 25 years, and is a Gemini and a bookworm. Her other titles include *The Good Karma Tarot*, *The Crystal Magic Tarot* (co-created with @bonearrow_), *Power, Purpose, Practice*, *Taroscopes* and *Card Of The Day Tarot*.

You can book your own personal reading with her at www.tarotbella.etsy.com or follow her at @mytarotbella.

Published in 2024 by Hardie Grant Books,
an imprint of Hardie Grant Publishing

Hardie Grant Books (London)
5th & 6th Floors
52–54 Southwark Street
London SE11UN

Hardie Grant Books (Melbourne)
Building 1, 658 Church Street
Richmond, Victoria 3121

hardiegrantbooks.com

British Library Cataloguing-in-Publication
Data. A catalogue record for this book
is available from the British Library.

The Cardless Tarot: Choose Your Own
Destiny Tarot Readings

ISBN: 978-1-78488-956-2

Publishing Director: Kate Pollard
Design: Claire Warner Studio
Copy Editor: Wendy Hobson
Proofreader: Leanne Burbridge
Production Controller: Gary Hayes
Colour Reproduction by p2d

Printed in China by C&C Offset Printing Co., Ltd.